PILI'S WALL

PHILIP
LEVINE

UNICORN
PRESS

For the stone masons & plasterers, the wind,
the sun, the rain, & my Pili, the
Spanish girlchild, all of you who
made this wall

& for Fran, who found it

I

Why me?

From this small hill
the river flows in March.
The soil gives grudgingly
grass, thyme, poppies,
thistles, cactus,
an olive grove climbing
the far hill, a row
of cedars shading the river.
What more?
A hobbled burro munching,
a she goat crying
for her young
who come crashing through
the tortured canyon.

What more?

II

I am the one
you never drew
the small sister
jumping rope
just within the circle
of the cypress

the lost dog
howling at shadows
and fleeing the chatter
of stones

the shepherd
alone and herdless
who came one afternoon
sweat running
from his eyes

seven jackdaws
soundless, until the sky
darkened
and there was
no place

III

Why am I here?
cries the gorse

Take these needles
crowding to your blood

these dense yellow mouths.
Take me, take me

the mother of spines
here under the olive

What can a child know,
says the moon

Look at her bones,
unbroken, and her teeth

May she sleep with stones
may she waken round a stone

Help me, help me, may she help me
flaps the gull

far from the sea and drunk
on the air of sweet grass

IV

Black circle of the sun.
Legs that carry nothing.
Arms that hold still.

Here is a face for you
who will not show
your face.
          I cut a smile
and give it to you, the rain
gives you tears.

Cold hills of February,
a dark smudge of sky
crashing like a wall.

Black circle of the sun,
you sweat and freeze
by turns.
          Bark back.
Your face peels down
to the black bone.

Spit your teeth
in the face
of creation.

V

This is my hand
reaching to you.

There is the dark island
where it never cries.

You're bigger than me
so put your hand
on my shoulder.

Now we're together
in the green tunnel
of the spring.

Jonquils, mustard,
new leaves dusting the light,
bone white buttons

that let the fields
lift easily
in the wind.

And my hand
in yours.

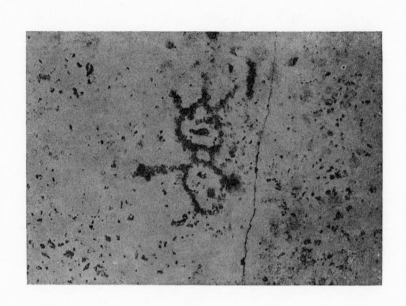

VI

This is me.
As I am.

There is no child
inside me. I
am a child.

I am inside me
squeezed tight, the
bright tongue

of the thistle
at night
or the quick eyes

of a rabbit
or the one eye
of fire.

With long black hair
I'm shaking inside
me, unfolding

like a tree
turning and
turning

like a hand
in water or a widow
lost on the road.

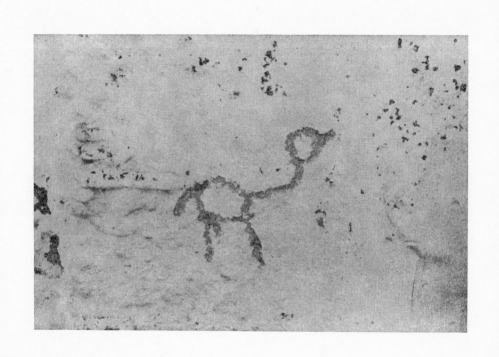

VII

I press my hand over
my mouth, I see nothing.

A blood bean
leaps at the foot of the wall

and I am with my face
turned in.

Out of lime
out of thatch, straw, stones

out of the years
of peeling and crying

Out of saying No
No to the barn swallow, No

to the hurled stone
No to the air

out of *you can't*
to the crying grain, *you won't*

to the lost river
of blackening ivy

out of blind
out of deaf, closed, still

I stand and stand and stand into
this wall.

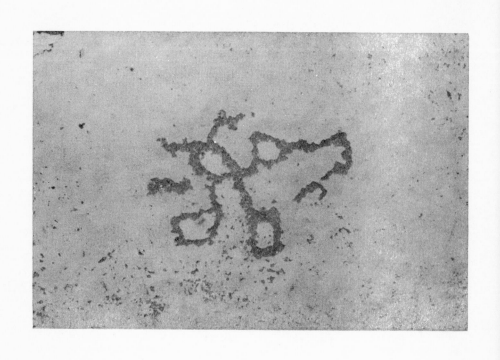

VIII

A simple dawn.

Inside the stalls
the pigs snuffle awake.
Light sifts through the thatch
crowning the dark odors,
the flies swing
in a rumor of birth
and the world starts.

From the far hill
of olives the wall is white
and perfect in the new sun.
The low houses of the poor
are squares of bread
dazzling the birds, and
no one can hear
the lost shoe
screaming in the weeds.

IX

Today I am
the wall, but once
I was seed

huddling between the grains
of stones, drawing a tongue

of salt into my blood, a fist
tightening into
a turnip

with one hard eye, until
a point of light
warmed

and gathering broke the dried crust
I was, and I was into
the air

the stiff back of me humping and
I breathed in
the green morning

like a row of windless corn
never to be
eaten.

X

Today I am Pili.
Palm Sunday, and I wait
in the cool morning

for my sisters, each one
in white to come
from the beaded door.

My brothers, restless, stone
the young pigs
into the road.

Below, the town trumpets
and I seem
to listen, I seem

to be this girl, this Pili, waiting
for children
with particular names

to gather before the chipped wall
and descend along
the goat trail,

and that is the sky up above, old father,
that seems to
be smiling down

on all of us with particular names, and that
is a field of cane,
there, across the road

where the pigs won't run
and a long dense shadow sleeps
at the roots.

750 copies of this first printing have been published, of which the first 50 are signed and numbered by the poet.

Patti Field hand-set the 14 Joanna type, and Rudy Villa-nueva hand-printed the book. 200 copies were hand-bound into full cloth by Gordon Thomsen.

PRINTED AT UNICORN PRESS